The Wiersbe
BIBLE STUDY SERIES

GENESIS 1–11

The
Wiersbe
BIBLE STUDY SERIES

Believing

the Simple

Truth of

God's Word

DAVID C COOK

transforming lives together

THE WIERSBE BIBLE STUDY SERIES: GENESIS 1—11
Published by David C Cook
4050 Lee Vance Drive
Colorado Springs, CO 80918 U.S.A.

Integrity Music Limited, a Division of David C Cook
Brighton, East Sussex BN1 2RE, England

The graphic circle C logo is a registered trademark of David C Cook.

All excerpts taken from *Be Basic*, second edition, published by David C Cook
in 2010 © 1998 Warren W. Wiersbe, ISBN 978-1-4347-6635-9.

ISBN 978-1-4347-0378-1
eISBN 978-0-7814-0857-8

© 2012 Warren W. Wiersbe

The Team: Steve Parolini, Karen Lee-Thorp, Amy Konyndyk,
Nick Lee, Jack Campbell, Karen Athen
Series Cover Design: John Hamilton Design
Cover Photo: Veer

Printed in the United States of America
First Edition 2012

7 8 9 10 11 12 13 14 15 16

051822

Contents

Introduction to Genesis 1–11

Basics

Whether you're learning to use a computer, drive a car, or climb a mountain, you have to start with the basics. As gifted as he was, even Mozart had to master the musical scales, and Shakespeare had to learn the English alphabet before he could write his great plays.

The book of Genesis is the "book of basics" because it's the "book of beginnings" in the Bible. To know Genesis is to know the fundamental truths—the basics—about God, the world, yourself and other people, law, sin, salvation, marriage, faith, and spiritual fulfillment. Inspired by the Spirit of God, Moses wrote Genesis and told us where we came from, why we're here, and what God expects us to do. Moses also explained how the Jewish nation began, the people through whom God would reveal Himself to the world, write the Bible, and ultimately give us our Savior, the Lord Jesus Christ.

God's Invitation

Genesis is the foundational book of the Bible, and the rest of Scripture is built on what Moses wrote. Genesis is quoted or referred to more than two hundred times in the New Testament, which means it's important for the New Testament Christian to understand its message.

As I read book catalogs and scan the shelves in bookstores, I'm fascinated to see the large number of books that have been published on Genesis, written by secular authors as well as by writers of the Judeo-Christian tradition. People are discovering in the ancient book of Genesis the basic truths we need to understand and apply in our fast-paced, social-networking world.

Genesis is God's invitation to you and me to *be basic*.

—*Warren W. Wiersbe*

How to Use This Study

This study is designed for both individual and small-group use. We've divided it into eight lessons—each references one or more chapters in Warren W. Wiersbe's commentary *Be Basic* (second edition, David C Cook, 2010). While reading *Be Basic* is not a prerequisite for going through this study, the additional insights and background Wiersbe offers can greatly enhance your study experience.

The **Getting Started** questions at the beginning of each lesson offer you an opportunity to record your first thoughts and reactions to the study text. This is an important step in the study process as those "first impressions" often include clues about what it is your heart is longing to discover.

The bulk of the study is found in the **Going Deeper** questions. These dive into the Bible text and, along with helpful excerpts from Wiersbe's commentary, help you examine not only the original context and meaning of the verses but also modern application.

Looking Inward narrows the focus down to your personal story. These intimate questions can be a bit uncomfortable at times, but don't shy away from honesty here. This is where you are asked to stand before the mirror of God's Word and look closely at what you see. It's the place to take

9

a good look at yourself in light of the lesson and search for ways in which you can grow in faith.

Going Forward is the place where you can commit to paper those things you want or need to do in order to better live out the discoveries you made in the Looking Inward section. Don't skip or skim through this. Take the time to really consider what practical steps you might take to move closer to Christ. Then share your thoughts with a trusted friend who can act as an encourager and accountability partner.

Finally, there is a brief **Seeking Help** section to close the lesson. This is a reminder for you to invite God into your spiritual-growth process. If you choose to write out a prayer in this section, come back to it as you work through the lesson and continue to seek the Holy Spirit's guidance as you discover God's will for your life.

Tips for Small Groups

A small group is a dynamic thing. One week it might seem like a group of close-knit friends. The next it might seem more like a group of uncomfortable strangers. A small-group leader's role is to read these subtle changes and adjust the tone of the discussion accordingly.

Small groups need to be safe places for people to talk openly. It is through shared wrestling with difficult life issues that some of the greatest personal growth is discovered. But in order for the group to feel safe, participants need to know it's okay *not* to share sometimes. Always invite honest disclosure, but never force someone to speak if he or she isn't comfortable doing so. (A savvy leader will follow up later with a group member who isn't comfortable sharing in a group setting to see if a one-on-one discussion is more appropriate.)

Have volunteers take turns reading excerpts from Scripture or from the commentary. The more each person is involved even in the mundane tasks, the more they'll feel comfortable opening up in more meaningful ways.

The leader should watch the clock and keep the discussion moving. Sometimes there may be more Going Deeper questions than your group can cover in your available time. If you've had a fruitful discussion, it's okay to move on without finishing everything. And if you think the group is getting bogged down on a question or has taken off on a tangent, you can simply say, "Let's go on to question 5." Be sure to save at least ten to fifteen minutes for the Going Forward questions.

Finally, soak your group meetings in prayer—before you begin, during as needed, and always at the end of your time together.

God Speaks
(GENESIS 1)

Before you begin ...
- *Pray for the Holy Spirit to reveal truth and wisdom as you go through this lesson.*
- *Read Genesis 1. This lesson references chapters 1 and 2 in* Be Basic. *It will be helpful for you to have your Bible and a copy of the commentary available as you work through this lesson.*

Getting Started

From the Commentary

What was happening before God spoke the universe into existence? That may seem like an impractical hypothetical question, like "How many angels can stand on the point of a pin?" but it isn't. After all, God doesn't act arbitrarily, and the fact that He created something suggests that He must have had some magnificent purposes in mind. What, then, was the situation before Genesis 1:1, and what does it teach us about God and ourselves?

—*Be Basic*, page 15

1. What can we know about things that preceded the events in Genesis? What does Genesis itself teach us about God's plan before the earth existed?

More to Consider: Moses said it best: "The secret things belong to the LORD *our God, but the things revealed belong to us and to our children forever, that we may follow all the words of this law" (Deut. 29:29). Read 1 Corinthians 13:9. How does this verse apply to our understanding of God's role in the universe prior to the creation of our world?*

2. Choose one verse or phrase from Genesis 1 that stands out to you. This could be something you're intrigued by, something that makes you uncomfortable, something that puzzles you, something that resonates with you, or just something you want to examine further. Write that here.

Going Deeper

From the Commentary

The first eleven chapters of Genesis deal with *humanity in general* and focus on four great events: creation (1—2), the fall of man and its consequences (3—5), the flood (6—9), and the rebellion at Babel (10—11). The rest of Genesis focuses on *Israel in particular* (12—50) and recounts the lives of four great men: Abraham (12:1—25:18), Isaac (25:19—27:46), Jacob (28—36), and Joseph (37—50). We call these men the "patriarchs" because they were the founding fathers of the Hebrew nation.

As you study Genesis, keep in mind that Moses didn't write a detailed history of each person or event. He recorded only those things that helped him achieve his purpose, which was to explain the origin of things, especially the origin of the Jewish nation. Genesis 1—11 is a record of failure, but with the call of Abraham, God made a new beginning. Man's sin had brought God's curse (3:14, 17; 4:11), but God's gracious covenant with Abraham brought blessing to the whole world (12:1–3).

—*Be Basic*, page 21

3. Why was it important for Moses to record the origin of things? What significance did this have to the Jewish nation? What "holes" are there in this record of life's beginning? How does the Bible fill in some of those holes for us?

From the Commentary

Some people call the president of the United States "the most powerful leader in the world," but more than one former president would disagree. Ex-presidents have confessed that their executive orders weren't always obeyed and that there wasn't much they could do about it.

For example, during President Nixon's first term in office, he ordered the removal of some ugly temporary buildings on the mall, eyesores that had been there since the World War I era, but it took many months before the order was obeyed. When journalists began writing about "the imperial presidency," Nixon called the whole idea "ludicrous." Presidents may speak and sign official orders, but that's no guarantee that anything will happen.

However, when God speaks, *something happens!* "For He spoke, and it was done; He commanded, and it stood fast" (Ps. 33:9 NKJV).

—*Be Basic*, page 27

4. What does God's power reveal about His character? In what ways do the events described in Genesis 1 inspire worship and awe? What should our response be to a God who has this kind of power and command over all living things?

From Today's World

The science of evolution has been taught in schools for decades. And for nearly as long, Christians have fought for the right to include the creation story in curriculum too. The battle has become a broader one in recent years as the theories of Intelligent Design have come to the fore, offering another (and not exclusively Christian) take on the beginning of everything. Opponents and proponents on all sides of the arguments are passionate about their beliefs, and this discussion isn't likely to abate anytime soon.

5. Why is there such passion in the evolution versus creation battle? How have the arguments changed over the years? What is science's response to creationism? What is Christianity's response to evolution? Can you land somewhere in between and still be a Christian? Explain.

From the Commentary

Three books of the Bible open with "beginnings": Genesis 1:1; Mark 1:1; and John 1:1. Each of these beginnings is important. "In the beginning was the Word" (John 1:1) takes us into eternity past when Jesus Christ, the living Word of God, existed as the eternal Son of God. John wasn't suggesting that Jesus had a beginning. Jesus Christ is the eternal Son of God who existed before all things because He made all things (John 1:3; Col. 1:16–17; Heb. 1:2). Therefore, John's "beginning" antedates Genesis 1:1.

The gospel of Mark opens with, "The beginning of the gospel of Jesus Christ, the Son of God." The message of the gospel didn't start with the ministry of John the Baptist, because the good news of God's grace was announced in Genesis 3:15. As Hebrews 11 bears witness, God's promise was believed by people throughout Old Testament history, and those who believed were saved. (See Gal. 3:1–9 and Rom. 4.) The ministry of John the Baptist, the forerunner of Jesus, was the beginning of the *proclamation* of the message concerning Jesus Christ of Nazareth (see Acts 1:21–22 and 10:37).

"In the beginning God created the heaven and the earth" (Gen. 1:1) refers to the dateless past when God brought the universe into existence out of nothing (Ps. 33:6; Rom. 4:17; Heb. 1:3). Genesis 1:1–2 is the *declaration* that God created the universe; the detailed *explanation* of the six days of God's creative work is given in the rest of the chapter.

—*Be Basic*, page 28

6. The Hebrew name for God in Genesis 1 is *Elohim*. This is a Hebrew word that emphasizes God's majesty and power. The New International Version and most other versions translate this word simply as "God." Underline the times God is called *Elohim* in Genesis 1. How is God's power revealed in

Genesis 1? Why is it particularly significant that God created the universe "out of nothing"? What has humankind created "out of nothing"?

From the Commentary

> God commanded the light to shine and then separated the light from the darkness. But how could there be light when the light-bearers aren't mentioned until the fourth day (Gen. 1:14–19)? Since we aren't told that this light came from any of the luminaries God created, it probably came from God Himself who is light (John 1:5) and wears light as a garment (Ps. 104:2; Hab. 3:3–4). The eternal city will enjoy endless light without the help of the sun or moon (Rev. 22:5), so why couldn't there be light at the beginning of time before the luminaries were made?
>
> Life as we know it could not exist without the light of the sun. Paul saw in this creative act the work of God in the new creation, the salvation of the lost. "For it is the God who commanded light to shine out of darkness, who has shone in our hearts to give the light of the knowledge of the glory of God in the face of Jesus Christ" (2 Cor. 4:6 NKJV).
>
> —*Be Basic*, pages 29–30

7. Light is a familiar theme throughout Scripture. How do the references to light in Genesis 1 set the stage for the way light is used later in God's Word? What does it mean that God Himself is light? Read John 1:4–5. What does this passage reveal about light?

From the Commentary

God put an expanse between the upper waters and the lower waters and made "heaven," what we know as "the sky." It seems that these waters were a vaporous "blanket" that covered the original creative mass. When separated from the landmass, the lower waters eventually became the ocean and the seas, and the upper waters played a part in the flood during Noah's day (Gen. 7:11–12; 9:11–15).

God gathered the waters and caused the dry land to appear, thus making "earth" and "seas." Israel's pagan neighbors believed all kinds of myths about the heavens, the earth, and the seas; but Moses made it clear that Elohim, the one true God, was Lord of them all. For the second time, God said that what He had done was "good" (v. 10; "light" being the first, v. 4). God's creation is still good, even though it travails because of sin (Rom.

8:20–22) and has been ravaged and exploited by sinful people.

—*Be Basic*, page 31

8. Why is it important that God calls His creation "good"? How does that affect the way we ought to treat it? How well are Christians caring for God's creation today? Is it possible to strip away the political from the spiritual when it comes to caring for the earth? Explain.

More to Consider: In the King James Version, the word translated "firmament" ("expanse" in NIV) means "to beat out." Why would Moses use this sort of word to describe the sky? How does his description of creation in Genesis contradict common pagan mythology that the sky was some kind of "solid covering"?

From the Commentary

Into the expanse of the sky God placed the heavenly bodies and assigned them their work: to divide the day and night and to provide "signs" to mark off days, years, and seasons. Light had already appeared on the first day, but now it was concentrated in these heavenly bodies.

God had created the sky and the waters, and now He filled them abundantly with living creatures. He made birds to fly in the sky and aquatic creatures to frolic in the seas. "O Lord, how manifold are Your works! In wisdom You have made them all. The earth is full of Your posses- sions—This great and wide sea, in which are innumerable teeming things, living things both small and great" (Ps. 104:24–25 NKJV).

—*Be Basic*, pages 32–33

9. How is the orderliness of God's creation significant? What does it teach us about God? Why did God choose to bless His creation? What did that blessing mean for the creation at that time? What does it mean for us today?

From the Commentary

> God had formed the sky and filled it with heavenly luminaries and flying birds. He had formed the seas and filled the waters with various aquatic creatures. Creation reaches its climax when on the sixth day He filled the land with animal life and then created the first man who, with his wife, would have dominion over the earth and its creatures.
>
> The creation of the first man is seen as a very special occasion, for there's a "consultation" prior to the event.
>
> —*Be Basic*, pages 33–34

10. Who is the "our" God refers to in Genesis 1:26? What does it mean that we are created in God's image? What does this tell us about God? About His intent for humankind?

Looking Inward

Take a moment to reflect on all that you've explored thus far in this study of Genesis 1. Review your notes and answers and think about how each of these things matters in your life today.

> *Tips for Small Groups: To get the most out of this section, form pairs or trios and have group members take turns answering these questions. Be honest and as open as you can in this discussion, but most of all, be encouraging and supportive of others. Be sensitive to those who are going through particularly difficult times and don't press for people to speak if they're uncomfortable doing so.*

11. Do you believe Genesis is a literal telling of the creation story? Why or why not? Is your faith strengthened or weakened by challenges to the literal belief of Genesis? What is the most important message for you in God's creation story?

12. What bothers you most about the biblical story of creation? What bothers you most about the science of evolution? Where do you stand in this discussion? How does this ongoing controversy affect you personally?

How can you use it as an opportunity to grow in faith? As an opportunity to share your faith with others?

13. How does being created in God's image affect the way you view yourself? How can you treat other people as bearers of God's image? Are non-Christians made in God's image? What about people who are disabled or even comatose? How should your answers to these questions affect the way you treat everyone you meet?

Going Forward

14. Think of one or two things that you have learned that you'd like to work on in the coming week. Remember that this is all about quality, not quantity. It's better to work on one specific area of life and do it well than to work on many and do poorly (or to be so overwhelmed that you simply don't try).

Do you want to treat other people more as bearers of God's image? Be specific. Go back through Genesis 1 and put a star next to the phrase or verse that is most encouraging to you. Consider memorizing this verse.

Real-Life Application Ideas: The first chapter of Genesis is the basis for our understanding of the beginning of life. However, it's often in stark contrast to the beliefs taught in school science classes. Do a little research to see what's being taught in your local schools. If you agree with the methods and content, send a note of thanks to the appropriate administrator. If you think they are lacking, send a letter expressing your thoughts (in a loving and kind way).

Seeking Help

15. Write a prayer below (or simply pray one in silence), inviting God to work on your mind and heart in those areas you've noted in the Going Forward section. Be honest about your desires and fears.

Notes for Small Groups:

- *Look for ways to put into practice the things you wrote in the Going Forward section. Talk with other group members about your ideas and commit to being accountable to one another.*

- *During the coming week, ask the Holy Spirit to continue to reveal truth to you from what you've read and studied.*

- *Before you start the next lesson, read Genesis 2. For more in-depth lesson preparation, read chapter 3, "First Things First," in* Be Basic.

First Things
(GENESIS 2)

Before you begin …
- *Pray for the Holy Spirit to reveal truth and wisdom as you go through this lesson.*
- *Read Genesis 2. This lesson references chapter 3 in* Be Basic. *It will be helpful for you to have your Bible and a copy of the commentary available as you work through this lesson.*

Getting Started

From the Commentary

If you could have been present to witness any event in Bible history, which event would you choose?

I once asked that question of several well-known Christian leaders, and the answers were varied: the crucifixion of Christ, the resurrection of Christ, the flood, Israel crossing the Red Sea, and even David slaying Goliath. But one of them said, "I would like to have been present when

God finished His creation. It must have been an awesome sight!"

Some scientists claim that if we could travel out into space fast enough and far enough, we could "catch up" with the light beams from the past and watch history unfold before our eyes. Perhaps the Lord will let us do that when we get to heaven. I hope so, because I would like to see the extraordinary events Moses described in Genesis 1 and 2.

—*Be Basic*, page 39

1. What are the "firsts" that Genesis 2 introduces to us? How do the events in Genesis 2 line up with the events in chapter 1? Why might some people think these are two different creation accounts?

2. Choose one verse or phrase from Genesis 2 that stands out to you. This could be something you're intrigued by, something that makes you uncomfortable, something that puzzles you, something that resonates with you, or just something you want to examine further. Write that here.

Going Deeper

From the Commentary

The word "Sabbath" isn't found in Genesis 2:1–3, but Moses is writing about the Sabbath, the seventh day of the week. The phrase "seventh day" is mentioned three times in verses 2–3. "Sabbath" comes from a Hebrew word *shabbat* that means "to cease working, to rest" and is related to the Hebrew word for "seven." We need to consider three different Sabbaths found in the Bible.

The first of these is the personal Sabbath of the Lord God (vv. 1–4). This first Sabbath didn't take place because God was tired from all His creative work, because God doesn't get weary (Isa. 40:28). God set apart the seventh day because His work of creation was finished and He was pleased and satisfied with what He had created. "And God saw everything that he had made, and, behold, it was very good" (Gen. 1:31).

—*Be Basic*, pages 39–40

3. What is distinctive about the seventh day of the creation week? Why did God make this a day of rest? What precedent does it set for His people? What message does it give us about God's own character?

More to Consider: It has been said that most people in our world are being "crucified between two thieves": the regrets of yesterday and the worries about tomorrow. How does God's creation story speak to this common modern malady? How does it teach us the importance of enjoying today?

From the Commentary

God had done many wonderful things during the six days of creation, but the climax of the creation week was God's "rest" after His work. As we shall see, God has sanctified work as well as rest, but it's rest that seems to be the greatest need in people's hearts today. Augustine was correct when he wrote, "Thou hast made us for Thyself, and our hearts are restless until they rest in Thee."

—*Be Basic*, page 41

4. What is God's message for us today in His decision to rest on the seventh day of creation? Why is it so difficult for people to rest today? Why is it important to be diligent about rest? How is rest different from worship? How is it a form of worship?

From Today's World

For many years, "blue" laws persisted in a number of states (and still do, though to a lesser degree than in years past). A blue law prohibited retail activity (usually the sale of alcohol) on Sundays. Originally the laws were put on the books to protect Sundays as a day of rest or a day of worship. Many businesses choose to close on Sundays for the same reason and, of course, government and public facilities are closed (in most cases) for the entire weekend.

5. Why were blue laws so popular years ago? What has made them less popular today? Why have they been the target of constitutional challenges? Do they contradict the idea of separation of church and state? Why or why not? How have Sundays changed over the years in America? In what ways are they still treated as days for rest and worship? In what ways are they not?

From the Commentary

> The nation of Israel eventually declined spiritually and didn't observe God's laws, including the Sabbath law, and they were ultimately punished for their disobedience (2 Chron. 36:14–21; Ezek. 20:1ff.; Isa. 58:13–14; Jer.

17:19–27). The northern kingdom of Israel was swallowed up by Assyria, and the Southern Kingdom of Judah was taken into captivity by Babylon.

By the time of the ministry of Jesus, the scribes and Pharisees had added their traditions to God's Word and turned the law in general and the Sabbath in particular into religious bondage. The few prohibitions found in Moses (Ex. 16:29; 35:2–3; Num. 15:32–36) were expanded into numerous regulations. Jesus, however, rejected their traditions and even performed miracles on the Sabbath! He said, "The sabbath was made for man, and not man for the sabbath" (Mark 2:27).

—*Be Basic*, page 42

6. The Bible shows how humans quickly moved away from God's intent in how they responded to the Sabbath. Why did God's people turn away from God's intent? What drew them away from observing the Sabbath? What draws people away from observing it today?

From the Commentary

> Hebrews 4 brings together God's creation rest (v. 4) and Israel's Canaan rest (v. 8) to teach us about the spiritual rest that believers have in Christ (vv. 9–11). When you trust Jesus Christ, you enter the "new creation" (2 Cor. 5:17) and into His spiritual rest (Matt. 11:28–30). You also enter into the spiritual inheritance He gives all who trust Him (Acts 20:32; Eph. 1:18; Col. 1:12). Believers are not under bondage to keep the law (Gal. 5:1) because the Holy Spirit fulfills the righteousness of the law in us as we yield to Him (Rom. 8:1–3).
>
> —*Be Basic*, page 43

7. Read Hebrews 4. What is this "spiritual rest"? Could God's people enter it before Jesus' time on earth? How do we experience it today?

From the Commentary

> Some Old Testament scholars have claimed that Genesis 2:4–14 is a second account of creation written by a

different author whose message conflicts with what's found in chapter 1. That theory isn't widely promoted today; for in these verses, Moses tells the same creation story but adds details that we need to know in order to understand events that happen later. Genesis 2:4 is the first of eleven "generation" statements that mark the progress of the story Moses wrote in the book of Genesis.

—*Be Basic*, page 44

8. What are some of the details Moses added to the creation story in chapter 2? Why are these details important to our understanding and interpretation of the creation story?

More to Consider: We don't have enough data to determine the exact location of the garden of Eden. Is it necessary to know the location of Eden to believe it existed? Why or why not? What is the most important takeaway from the garden of Eden story? How can we apply this to our lives even apart from evidence to prove its literal existence?

From the Commentary

> A covenant is a binding arrangement between two or more parties that governs their relationship. The word *command* is introduced in Genesis 2:16–17 because it's God who makes the terms of the agreement. God is the Creator and man is the creature, a "royal tenant" in God's wonderful world, so God has the right to tell the man what he can and cannot do. God didn't ask for Adam's advice; He simply gave him His commandment.
>
> God had given great honor and privilege to Adam in making him His vice-regent on the earth (1:28), but with privilege always comes responsibility. The same divine Word that brought the universe into being also expresses God's love and will to Adam and Eve and their descendants (Ps. 33:11). Obedience to this Word would keep them in the sphere of God's fellowship and approval. All God's commands are good commands and bring good things to those who obey them (Ps. 119:39; Prov. 6:20–23). "And his commands are not burdensome" (1 John 5:3 NIV).
>
> —*Be Basic*, page 46

9. What responsibilities did God give Adam after placing him on the earth? Why do you think obedience is such a key aspect of the relationship between God and people? How is obedience a good command from God? Why is it so hard to live out?

From the Commentary

> At the close of the sixth day of creation, God had surveyed
> everything He had made and pronounced it "very good"
> (Gen. 1:31). But now God says that there's something in
> His wonderful world that is not good: The man is alone.
> In fact, in the Hebrew text, the phrase "not good" is at the
> beginning of the Lord's statement in 2:18.
>
> —*Be Basic*, page 47

10. What was "not good" about Adam's solitude? What more could he
want? Why do you think the Genesis account tells of God's decision to give
Adam a helper instead of merely stating, "God made man and woman and
all was good"? Was this the first marriage? Explain.

Looking Inward

Take a moment to reflect on all that you've explored thus far in this study
of Genesis 2. Review your notes and answers and think about how each of
these things matters in your life today.

Tips for Small Groups: To get the most out of this section, form pairs or trios and have group members take turns answering these questions. Be honest and as open as you can in this discussion, but most of all, be encouraging and supportive of others. Be sensitive to those who are going through particularly difficult times and don't press for people to speak if they're uncomfortable doing so.

11. What are the most important elements of the creation story to you? What events or details encourage you? What events or details confound you? How does the creation story matter in your life today? If it doesn't, should it? Why?

12. Do you have a "Sabbath" in your faith life? If so, what does it look like? In what ways is it like what God practiced in the creation story? What are some ways you could make your Sabbath more restful?

13. The first marriage is found in Genesis 2. What strikes you as significant about God's introduction of woman? Is it possible to read too much into this story? What overall message do you get from God's decision to give woman as a gift to man? Does it say more about God or about humankind?

Going Forward

14. Think of one or two things that you have learned that you'd like to work on in the coming week. Remember that this is all about quality, not quantity. It's better to work on one specific area of life and do it well than to work on many and do poorly (or to be so overwhelmed that you simply don't try).

Do you want to be more deliberate about practicing Sabbath rest? Be specific. Go back through Genesis 2 and put a star next to the phrase or verse that is most encouraging to you. Consider memorizing this verse.

Real-Life Application Ideas: Take a close look at your weekly schedule. Do you make time for Sabbath rest? What would your schedule look like if you did? Start being intentional about Sabbath over the course of the next few weeks. As you do, look for ways to embrace this time of rest as a true time to meditate on all the gifts God has given you.

Seeking Help

15. Write a prayer below (or simply pray one in silence), inviting God to work on your mind and heart in those areas you've noted in the Going Forward section. Be honest about your desires and fears.

Notes for Small Groups:

- *Look for ways to put into practice the things you wrote in the Going Forward section. Talk with other group members about your ideas and commit to being accountable to one another.*

- *During the coming week, ask the Holy Spirit to continue to reveal truth to you from what you've read and studied.*

- *Before you start the next lesson, read Genesis 3. For more in-depth lesson preparation, read chapters 4 and 5, "This Is My Father's World—or Is It?" and "Perils in Paradise," in* Be Basic.

Paradise Lost
(GENESIS 3)

Before you begin ...
- *Pray for the Holy Spirit to reveal truth and wisdom as you go through this lesson.*
- *Read Genesis 3. This lesson references chapters 4 and 5 in Be Basic. It will be helpful for you to have your Bible and a copy of the commentary available as you work through this lesson.*

Getting Started

From the Commentary

"Let all the earth fear the Lord; let all the people of the world revere him. For he spoke, and it came to be; he commanded, and it stood firm" (Ps. 33:8–9 NIV).

Creation reveals the existence of God, the power of God, and the wisdom of God. That this complex universe should appear by accident out of nothing from a "big bang" is as probable as the works of Shakespeare resulting from an explosion in a printing plant. Only a God of power could create something out of nothing, and only a God of wisdom could make it function as it does. The scientist is only thinking God's thoughts after Him and discovering the laws that God built into His world at creation.

—*Be Basic*, page 55

1. What are some of the laws God built into creation? How do they affirm God's role? Read Psalm 19:1; Mark 10:6; 13:19; Romans 1:20, 22; 2 Peter 3:4. How do these passages affirm God's role in creation?

More to Consider: Read Romans 1:18–32. What does this passage tell us about how humankind moved from worshipping God to worshipping false gods and dead idols? Why is it significant that people didn't start by worshipping nature first?

2. Choose one verse or phrase from Genesis 3 that stands out to you. This could be something you're intrigued by, something that makes you uncomfortable, something that puzzles you, something that resonates with you, or just something you want to examine further. Write that here.

Going Deeper

From the Commentary

> When God gave the first man and woman dominion over creation (Gen. 1:26–30), He put them and their descendants under obligation to value His gifts and use them carefully for His glory. God created everything for His glory and pleasure (Rev. 4:11) as well as for our enjoyment and use (1 Tim. 6:17; Acts 17:24–28), and we must always see ourselves as stewards in God's world. To destroy creation and waste its bounties is to sin against God.
>
> In this universe, we have God, people, and the things that God made, among them water, land, animal and plant life, air, and vast resources underground. We're commanded to worship God, love people, and use things for the glory of God and the good of others. When this divine order becomes confused, then God's creation suffers.
>
> —*Be Basic*, page 56

3. What does it look like to "use things for the glory of God and the good of others" when it comes to the earth and all that's in it? What does it mean that God gave us dominion over the earth? What's the relationship between dominion over and caring for the earth?

From the Commentary

> The agnostic and atheist have every right to worry because (as someone has said) "they have no invisible means of support." To them, the universe is a self-made impersonal machine, not the creation of a wise God and loving Father. But Christian believers see creation as their Father's world. They call the Creator "Father," and they trust Him with their lives, their circumstances, and their future.
>
> Everything in nature praises the Lord and looks to Him for whatever they need. "These all wait for You, that You may give them their food in due season" (Ps. 104:27 NKJV). There's no evidence that robins get ulcers or that rabbits have nervous breakdowns.
>
> —*Be Basic*, pages 57–58

4. How does nature praise the Lord? What does it mean to trust God to provide? What does Genesis teach us about God's provision?

From Today's World

There are only a few topics more controversial these days than the environment. Politics has essentially divided the argument along party lines, but concerns about God's creation run deeper than politics. Whatever you believe about resources—renewable and otherwise—it's clear that human-kind hasn't always been a good caretaker of the planet and its inhabitants.

5. Why are environmental issues so contentious? Why do people tend to politicize them? What is God's charge to His people concerning the earth and all within it? How can Christians lead the charge to care properly and appropriately for God's creation?

From the Commentary

God is the Creator, and He's given His creatures a book that helps them understand who He is, how He works, and what He wants them to do. It's a book of precepts to obey, promises to believe, and principles to understand. It's also a book about real people, some of whom obeyed the Lord and some who didn't, and from the experiences of these people, we can learn a great deal about what to avoid on the path of life.

We should by all means learn all we can, but everything we learn must be tested by the Word of God. American physicist and Nobel Prize recipient Robert A. Millikan said, "I consider an intimate knowledge of the Bible an indispensable qualification of a well-educated man." Yale University professor William Lyon Phelps agreed when he said, "Everyone who has a thorough knowledge of the Bible may truly be called educated … I believe knowledge of the Bible without a college course is more valuable than a college course without the Bible."

If you believe that God is your Creator, and that you're living in His universe, then listen to what He has to say and obey it, for that's the secret of true fulfillment and success (Josh. 1:7–9).

—*Be Basic*, page 63

6. What do you learn about God from His creation? From the manner in which He created everything? What do the first chapters of Genesis teach us about God's hope for his best creation: humans?

From the Commentary

> If Genesis 3 were not in the Bible, there would be no Bible
> as we know it. Why? Because the rest of Scripture docu-
> ments the sad consequences of Adam's sin and explains
> what God in His grace has done to rescue us. By grasping
> the basic truths of this important chapter, you can better
> understand Paul's discussion of justification in Romans 5,
> his teaching in 1 Timothy 2:8–15 about men and women
> in the church, and his explanation in 1 Corinthians 15 of
> the future resurrection.
>
> —*Be Basic*, page 67

7. How did Adam's disobedience bring sin into the human race? Why
doesn't the Bible give us an explanation for the existence of Satan before
the fall of humankind? What would have happened to the Christian faith
if the fall had never occurred? How did God use the story of the fall to set
the stage for His ultimate offer of grace?

From the Commentary

> A temptation is an opportunity to accomplish a good thing in a bad way. It's a good thing to pass a school examination but a bad thing to do it by cheating. It's a good thing to pay your bills but a bad thing to steal the money for the payments. In essence, Satan said to Eve: "I can give you something that you need and want. You can have it now and enjoy it, and best of all, there won't be any painful consequences. What an opportunity!"
>
> —*Be Basic*, page 68

8. Review Genesis 3:1–5. What steps did Satan take to tempt Eve? Why would God allow Eve to be tempted in the first place? What are some other good things that humans have attempted to accomplish in a bad way?

More to Consider: What is "the lie" (singular) that has ruled civilization since the fall of humankind? It's the belief that men and women can be their own gods and live for the creation, instead of for the Creator, without suffering any consequences. Read the following verses: Ephesians 2:1–3; Matthew 7:13–23; Revelation 20:10–15. What do these verses tell us about the fate of those who believe that lie?

From the Commentary

Humans are so constructed that they must believe something; if they don't believe the truth, then they'll eventually believe lies (2 Thess. 2:10). But if they believe lies, they will have to suffer the consequences that always come when people reject God's truth.

How God appeared to our first parents when they fellowshipped with Him in the garden isn't explained to us. He probably assumed a temporary body that veiled His glory, as He would do when He visited Abraham many years later (Gen. 18:1ff.).

—*Be Basic*, pages 71, 74

9. Why doesn't the Bible tell us more about how God revealed Himself to Adam and Eve in the garden? Is it critical to know how He interacted with them? Why or why not? How can this mystery actually encourage believers today as they pursue their relationships with God?

From the Commentary

God's love for sinners in no way eliminates His holy hatred for sin, for while it's true that "God is love" (1 John 4:8, 16), it's also true that "God is light" (1:5). A holy God must deal with sin, for the good of the sinner and for the glory of His name.

For the sake of His own character and law, God must judge sin, but for the sake of His beloved Son, God is willing to forgive sin. Remember, Jesus is the Lamb "slain from the foundation of the world" (Rev. 13:8; see Acts 2:23; 4:27–28), so that God had already made provision for forgiveness and salvation.

—*Be Basic*, pages 75, 77–78

10. Review Genesis 3:14–24. What is God's response to Adam and Eve's sin? What does this reveal to us about God? Why did God offer Adam and Eve a second chance after they disobeyed Him?

Looking Inward

Take a moment to reflect on all that you've explored thus far in this study of Genesis 3. Review your notes and answers and think about how each of these things matters in your life today.

Tips for Small Groups: To get the most out of this section, form pairs or trios and have group members take turns answering these questions. Be honest and as open as you can in this discussion, but most of all, be encouraging and supportive of others. Be sensitive to those who are going through particularly difficult times and don't press for people to speak if they're uncomfortable doing so.

11. What are some ways you're caring for God's creation? What are some ways you're being irresponsible with it? What can you do to show more love for God's creation? How do you balance this with other aspects of your faith life?

12. What are some ways you struggle with obeying God like Adam and Eve did? Why is it so hard to remain obedient to God? What are you most thankful for when you think about the garden of Eden story?

13. In what ways do you experience the effects of the fall? Is it helpful for you to know that painful toil (as opposed to the joyous work in the garden) and strife between the sexes aren't part of God's original intent? How do you think you should deal with life in a fallen world?

Going Forward

14. Think of one or two things that you have learned that you'd like to work on in the coming week. Remember that this is all about quality, not quantity. It's better to work on one specific area of life and do it well than to work on many and do poorly (or to be so overwhelmed that you simply don't try).

Do you want to seek God's help to be obedient to His will? Be specific. Go back through Genesis 3 and put a star next to the phrase or verse that is most encouraging to you. Consider memorizing this verse.

Real-Life Application Ideas: The book of Genesis tells us that God's creation is good. It's our responsibility to care for that creation. Make a list of ways you can celebrate and care for God's creation in your daily life. Then do those things.

Seeking Help

15. Write a prayer below (or simply pray one in silence), inviting God to work on your mind and heart in those areas you've noted in the Going Forward section. Be honest about your desires and fears.

Notes for Small Groups:
- *Look for ways to put into practice the things you wrote in the Going Forward section. Talk with other group members about your ideas and commit to being accountable to one another.*
- *During the coming week, ask the Holy Spirit to continue to reveal truth to you from what you've read and studied.*
- *Before you start the next lesson, read Genesis 4:1–24. For more in-depth lesson preparation, read chapter 6, "In Center Stage—Cain," in* Be Basic.

Cain

(GENESIS 4:1–24)

Before you begin ...
- *Pray for the Holy Spirit to reveal truth and wisdom as you go through this lesson.*
- *Read Genesis 4:1–24. This lesson references chapter 6 in Be Basic. It will be helpful for you to have your Bible and a copy of the commentary available as you work through this lesson.*

Getting Started

From the Commentary

"All the world's a stage, and all the men and women merely players," wrote Shakespeare. "They have their exits and their entrances, and one man in his time plays many parts."

Remember those familiar words from English Lit 101? Shakespeare was right: We have many roles to play in life as from time to time we relate to various people and confront different circumstances. The important thing is that we let God write the script, choose the cast, and direct the action. If we disregard Him and try to produce the drama ourselves, the story will have a tragic ending.

That's what ruined Cain, the first human baby born on the stage of Planet Earth: He ignored God's script, "did his own thing," and made a mess out of it. Genesis 4 focuses the spotlight on Cain; he's mentioned sixteen times, and seven times Abel is identified as "his [Cain's] brother." As you consider Cain's life and some of the roles he played, you will better understand how important it is for us to know God and do His will.

—*Be Basic*, page 81

1. What are some of the ways Cain ignored God's script? How do we ignore His script today? What are the best ways to be sure we follow the plan God has for us?

2. Choose one verse or phrase from Genesis 4:1–24 that stands out to you. This could be something you're intrigued by, something that makes you

uncomfortable, something that puzzles you, something that resonates with you, or just something you want to examine further. Write that here.

Going Deeper

From the Commentary

> God commanded our first parents to "be fruitful, and multiply, and replenish the earth" (Gen. 1:28), and they obeyed this mandate (5:4). While it's true that the building of a family isn't the only purpose for marriage, and not every marriage is blessed with children, it's also true that children are a precious gift from God (33:5; 48:9; Ps. 127:3) and should be welcomed with joy.
>
> —*Be Basic*, page 82

3. Why were families so important in the earliest days of history? How has that changed over the years? What might the Jewish people in the Old Testament feel about today's abortion statistics?

More to Consider: The name "Cain" sounds like the Hebrew word for "acquired." Eve praised God for helping her through her first pregnancy. Her second pregnancy brought Abel into the world. His name means "breath" and is the word translated "vanity" at least thirty-eight times in Ecclesiastes. What does each of these names teach us about God? About the first children? About ourselves?

From the Commentary

Genesis is a "family book" and has a good deal to say about brothers. Being the firstborn son, Cain was special, but because of his sin, he lost everything and Seth took his place (Gen. 4:25). Ishmael was Abraham's firstborn, but God bypassed him and chose Isaac. Esau was Isaac's firstborn son, but he was rejected for Jacob, and Jacob's firstborn son Reuben was replaced by Joseph's two sons (49:3–4; 1 Chron. 5:1–2). In fact, God even rearranged the birth order of Joseph's sons (Gen. 48:8–22).

—*Be Basic*, page 82

4. Why did firstborn sons have special status in Old Testament times? Are firstborns still given special treatment today? Why or why not? What does it say about God that He sometimes changed the rules to honor others with the blessing usually reserved for the firstborn?

From Today's World

Sibling rivalry hasn't disappeared in the thousands of years since the first brothers walked this earth. In some ways it's gotten even worse. In a culture that celebrates success above all else (and defines that success according to dollars and cents), siblings are often pitted against each other in a race to the top. Whether it's competing for jobs or trying to outdo one another in social activism, siblings continue to wrestle with the same selfish desires and jealousy Cain acted upon at the dawn of humankind.

5. Why do siblings continue to do battle in an enlightened society? Why hasn't humanity learned from its many mistakes? What causes siblings to go against each other? What does this say about the state of the family in society today? How is that different from the days of Cain and Abel? How is it the same? What are some ways to shore up the family in order to avoid or minimize sibling rivalry?

From the Commentary

> As his sons grew older, Adam put them to work in the fields, and it became evident over the years that each boy had his own interests and skills. Cain became a farmer and Abel became a shepherd; the first of many shepherds

found in the Bible, including Abraham, Isaac, Jacob and his sons, Moses, and David.

Adam certainly taught his sons why they worked: It was a part of God's creation mandate, and they were colaborers with God (Gen. 1:26–31). Work isn't a punishment from God because of sin, for Adam had work to do in the garden before he and his wife yielded to Satan's temptation. The biblical approach to work is that we are privileged to cooperate with God by using His creation gifts for the good of people and the glory of God.

—*Be Basic*, page 83

6. In what ways is work a blessing from God? Read Colossians 3:22–23; 1 Thessalonians 4:11–12; Ecclesiastes 9:10. What do these passages tell us about the purpose and importance of work?

From the Commentary

Adam and Eve had learned to worship God during those wonderful days in the garden before sin had brought its curse to their lives and to the ground. Certainly they taught their children about the Lord and the importance of worshipping Him. Workers need to be worshippers or they may become idolaters, focusing on the gifts and not the Giver, and forgetting that God gives the power to work and gain wealth (Deut. 8:10–20).

When God clothed Adam and Eve with the skins of animals (Gen. 3:21), perhaps He taught them about sacrifices and the shedding of blood, and they would have passed this truth along to their children.

—*Be Basic*, page 84

7. Review Genesis 4:3–7. What do you think worship looked like for the first humans? How did they learn how to worship? Why is it important for God's people to worship Him? Why is it important to God?

From the Commentary

The fact that people attend religious meetings and participate in church activities is no proof that they're true believers. It's possible to have "a form of godliness" but never experience its saving power (2 Tim. 3:5). "These people come near to me with their mouth and honor me with their lips, but their hearts are far from me" (Isa. 29:13 NIV; Matt. 15:8). The most costly sacrifices apart from the submission of the heart can never make the worshipper right before God (Ps. 51:16–17).

—*Be Basic*, page 85

8. How was "the way of Cain" the way of self-will and unbelief? (See Jude v. 11.) How did Cain react when God rejected his offering? How did God try to help Cain after he became angry? What does this tell us about God? About people?

More to Consider: Read Ephesians 4:27. How is what Paul wrote similar to God's warning to Cain that temptation was like a crouching beast? What does it mean to "give the devil a foothold"? How did Cain do this? How do believers do this today?

From the Commentary

We can't separate our relationship with God from our relationship with our brothers and sisters. (That includes our natural brothers and sisters as well as our brothers and sisters in the Lord.) An unforgiving spirit, such as possessed Cain, hinders worship and destroys our fellowship with God and God's people (Matt. 5:21–26; 6:14–15). It's better that we interrupt our worship and get right with a brother than to pollute our sacrifice because we have a bad spirit within.

—*Be Basic*, page 85

9. Why is anger such a dangerous emotion? How did anger infect Cain's life? What did Jesus teach about anger? (See Matt. 5:21–26.) How does anger continue to hurt people today?

From the Commentary

A vagabond has no home; a fugitive is running from home; a stranger is away from home; but a pilgrim is heading home. "I have set before you life and death, blessing and cursing: therefore choose life" (Deut. 30:19). Cain made the wrong choice, and instead of being a pilgrim in life, he became a stranger and a fugitive, wandering the land.

God kept His Word and protected Cain as he wandered. One day he found a place that seemed right for him to settle down, and he decided to build a city. The earth wouldn't yield its strength to Cain's labor as a farmer, but Cain could labor and build *on the earth* and succeed. However, Cain never ceased to be a fugitive, for the name of the land where he settled means "wandering." His citizenship wasn't in heaven (Phil. 3:20–21 NKJV), nor did he have any hope to reach the heavenly city (Heb. 11:9–16).

—*Be Basic*, pages 87–89

10. Review Genesis 4:11–24. Why did Cain become a wanderer? How did God protect him anyway? What was the only "heaven" Cain would know? How might Cain have changed his fortune, even after murdering Abel? What does this story teach us about the danger of stubbornness?

Looking Inward

Take a moment to reflect on all that you've explored thus far in this study of Genesis 4:1–24. Review your notes and answers and think about how each of these things matters in your life today.

Tips for Small Groups: To get the most out of this section, form pairs or trios and have group members take turns answering these questions. Be honest and as open as you can in this discussion, but most of all, be encouraging and supportive of others. Be sensitive to those who are going through particularly difficult times and don't press for people to speak if they're uncomfortable doing so.

11. Family was important to the earliest humans not just because it meant survival but also because it was important to God. Think about your family situation. What are some ways you have valued your family? What are some ways you have devalued them? Whatever your background or current situation, what does it look like to love your family?

12. Cain didn't listen to God's offer of guidance. When have you intentionally ignored God? What was the result of that disobedience?

What are some ways you listen for God's voice? How do you respond if you don't like what you hear? What role does trust play in listening to God?

13. Describe a time when you let anger get the best of you. What was the result? Was anyone hurt by your anger? How did you resolve that situation? What are some good ways to avoid letting anger control you?

Going Forward

14. Think of one or two things that you have learned that you'd like to work on in the coming week. Remember that this is all about quality, not quantity. It's better to work on one specific area of life and do it well than to work on many and do poorly (or to be so overwhelmed that you simply don't try).

Do you need to work on loving your family more? Overcome anger issues? Be specific. Go back through Genesis 4:1–24 and put a star next to the phrase or verse that is most encouraging to you. Consider memorizing this verse.

Real-Life Application Ideas: Think about any unresolved issues in your family, whether with a parent, sibling, or even a child. What is the root cause of that conflict? What would it look like for you to approach the situation humbly and out of love? How might God direct you to resolve that issue? Spend time thinking about this by praying and studying God's Word on appropriate topics. Then, if possible, take action to resolve differences in order to avoid letting anger rule the relationship.

Seeking Help

15. Write a prayer below (or simply pray one in silence), inviting God to work on your mind and heart in those areas you've noted in the Going Forward section. Be honest about your desires and fears.

Notes for Small Groups:

- *Look for ways to put into practice the things you wrote in the Going Forward section. Talk with other group members about your ideas and commit to being accountable to one another.*
- *During the coming week, ask the Holy Spirit to continue to reveal truth to you from what you've read and studied.*
- *Before you start the next lesson, read Genesis 4:25— 7:24. For more in-depth lesson preparation, read chapters 7 and 8, "When the Outlook Is Bleak, Try the Uplook" and "One Man's Faith, One Man's Family," in* Be Basic.

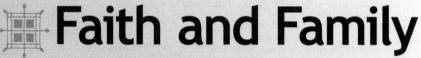

Faith and Family

(GENESIS 4:25—7:24)

Before you begin …

- *Pray for the Holy Spirit to reveal truth and wisdom as you go through this lesson.*
- *Read Genesis 4:25—7:24. This lesson references chapters 7 and 8 in* Be Basic. *It will be helpful for you to have your Bible and a copy of the commentary available as you work through this lesson.*

Getting Started

From the Commentary

Genesis 5 is the first genealogy in Scripture and introduces "the book of the generations of Adam" (v. 1). Ten generations are listed here, from Adam to Noah, just as ten generations are listed from Shem to Abraham in "the generations of Shem" (11:10–26). Eight times in Genesis 5 you find the melancholy phrase "and he died," for death was now reigning over mankind because of Adam's sin (Rom. 5:12–17, 21). Sin and death still reign today, but through Jesus Christ we can "reign in life" (v. 17, see also v. 21).

In Bible history, very often the birth of a baby has made the difference between defeat and victory for God's people. During the Jews' difficult years in Egypt, Moses was born and became the liberator of his people (Ex. 2:1–10). When the lamp of prophecy was burning very low, Samuel was born to bring Israel back to God's Word (1 Sam. 1—3), and when the kingdom was disintegrating under Saul, God sent a son to Jesse whom he named David, the man God had chosen to be the next king (Ruth 4:18–22; 1 Sam. 16). At a very low point in Jewish history, by the grace of God, one little boy continued the messianic line from David (2 Kings 11:1–3). In spite of Satan's attacks and the disobedience of His people, God was faithful to work so that His promise of a Redeemer would be fulfilled.

—*Be Basic*, page 94

1. Circle or underline all the references to death in Genesis 5. How might these people, unaccustomed to death, have felt about the passing of generations? What might it have taught them about how to live? About the importance of family?

More to Consider: Seth was 105 years old when his son Enosh was born (Gen. 5:6). "Enosh" comes from a Hebrew word that means "frail, weak." Why might Seth have chosen this name in this period of history? What does this tell us about humankind?

2. Choose one verse or phrase from Genesis 4:25—7:24 that stands out to you. This could be something you're intrigued by, something that makes you uncomfortable, something that puzzles you, something that resonates with you, or just something you want to examine further. Write that here.

Going Deeper

From the Commentary

> The sobering phrase "and he died" isn't used of Enoch, because Enoch is one of two men in Scripture who never died. Both Enoch and Elijah were taken to heaven alive (2 Kings 2:1–11). Some students see in Enoch's pre-flood "rapture" a picture of the church being taken to heaven before God sends tribulation on the earth (1 Thess. 4:13—5:11).

> It was "by faith" that Enoch was taken to heaven (Heb.

11:5). He believed God, walked with God, and went to be with God, which is an example for all of us to follow. Imagine how difficult it must have been to walk with God during those years before the flood, when vice and violence were prevalent and only a remnant of people believed God (Gen. 6:5).... In his day, the judgment of the flood did come, but the judgment Enoch was announcing will occur when Jesus Christ returns, leading the armies of heaven and condemning Satan and his hosts (Rev. 19:11ff.). Enoch's life and witness remind us that it's possible to be faithful to God in the midst of "a crooked and perverse nation" (Phil. 2:15).

—*Be Basic*, page 97

3. Read Jude verses 14–15. What does this passage reveal about Enoch's life of faith? How was Enoch able to live a godly life in the midst of a world filled with perversion? What can Enoch's life teach us about how to live today?

From the Commentary

After chapter 3, Satan isn't mentioned by name in Genesis, but he and his demonic hosts are at work doing their utmost to keep the promised Redeemer from being born. This was Satan's purpose throughout all of Old Testament history. After all, he didn't want to have his head crushed by the Savior (3:15)! God had declared war on Satan and the deceiver intended to fight back.

One of Satan's most successful devices is *compromise*. If he can delude God's people into abandoning their privileged position of separation from sin and communion with God, then he can corrupt them and lead them into sin. He did this to Israel in the land of Moab (Num. 25; Ps. 106:28–31) and also after they had conquered the land of Canaan (Judg. 2; Ps. 106:34–48). The prophets warned the Jewish people not to compromise with the idolatrous worship of the pagans around them, but their warnings weren't heeded, and the nation experienced shameful defeat at the hands of their enemies.

What was Satan's plan for defeating God's people in Noah's day? To entice the godly line of Seth ("the sons of God") to mix with the ungodly line of Cain ("the daughters of men") and thus abandon their devotion to the Lord.

—*Be Basic*, pages 98–99

4. How is the way Satan wanted to entice the godly people to mix with the ungodly similar to the way he has tempted people ever since? Read Romans 12:2; 2 Corinthians 6:14—7:1; James 4:4; 1 John 2:15–17. What does worldly compromise look like today? Read 1 Corinthians 11:32. What does following Satan's temptation lead to?

From the Commentary

> Some interpreters view Genesis 6:1–7 as an invasion of fallen angels who cohabited with women and produced a race of giants. But as interesting as the theory is, it creates more problems than it solves, not the least of which is the union of sexless spirit beings with flesh and blood humans. Even if such unions did occur, could there be offspring and why would they be giants? And how did these "giants" (Nephilim, "fallen ones") survive the flood (v. 4; Num. 13:31–33), or was there a second invasion of fallen angels after the flood?
>
> The term "sons of God" does refer to angels in Job 1:6; 2:1; 38:7, but these are *unfallen* angels faithfully serving God. Even if fallen angels could make themselves appear in human bodies, why would they want to marry

women and settle down on earth? Certainly their wives and neighbors would detect something different about them and this would create problems. Furthermore, the emphasis in Genesis 6 is on the sin of *man* and not the rebellion of angels. The word "man" is used nine times in verses 1–7, and God states clearly that the judgment was coming because of what humans had done. "And God saw that the wickedness of man was great in the earth" (v. 5).

—*Be Basic*, page 99

5. What makes Genesis 6:1–7 difficult to interpret? Why might some confuse the message here to be more about fallen angels than about humans? Why is it important that this passage is actually talking more about the sins of humans?

From the Commentary

The only way people can be saved from God's wrath is through God's grace (Eph. 2:8–9), but grace isn't God's reward for a good life: It's God's response to saving faith.

"By faith Noah, being divinely warned of things not yet seen, moved with godly fear, prepared an ark for the saving of his household" (Heb. 11:7 NKJV). True faith involves the whole of the inner person: The mind understands God's warning, the heart fears for what is coming, and the will acts in obedience to God's Word.

To understand God's truth but not act upon it is not biblical faith; it's only intellectual assent to religious truth. To be emotionally aroused without comprehending God's message isn't faith, because true faith is based on an understanding of the truth (Matt. 13:18–23). To have the mind enlightened and the heart stirred but not act in obedience to the message is not faith, for "faith without works is dead" (James 2:14–26). The mind, heart, and will are all involved in true biblical faith.

—*Be Basic*, pages 100–1

6. Why is Noah's "saved by grace" story so significant to the bigger picture of God's plan? How was it a precursor to the salvation Jesus brings? Review Hebrews 11. How have each of these notable Bible characters been saved by grace? How do we, like Noah, find "favor in the eyes of the LORD" (Gen. 6:8)?

From the Commentary

Noah wasn't a minor character in the story of redemption; he's mentioned fifty times in eleven different books of the Bible.

Noah was a righteous man (Gen. 6:9; 7:1). Genesis 6:9 is the first time the word "righteous" is used in the Bible, but Noah's righteousness is also mentioned in other places (Ezek. 14:14, 20; Heb. 11:7; 2 Peter 2:5). Noah's righteousness didn't come from his good works; his good works came because of his righteousness. Like Abraham, his righteousness was God's gift in response to his personal faith. Both Abraham and Noah believed God's Word and it was "counted ... to [them] for righteousness" (Gen. 15:6; see Heb. 11:7; Rom. 4:9ff.; Gal. 3:1ff.).

The only righteousness God will accept is the righteousness of Jesus Christ, His Son (2 Cor. 5:21), and the only way people can receive that righteousness is by admitting their sins and trusting Jesus Christ to save them (Rom. 3:19–30; Gal. 2:16).

—*Be Basic*, page 106

7. Where did Noah likely learn about true righteousness? (See Gen. 5:28–29.) What does this tell us about the importance of passing wisdom on to our children?

From the Commentary

> Noah's great-grandfather Enoch had "walked with God" and was suddenly taken to heaven and rescued from the impending judgment of the flood (Gen. 5:24). Noah walked with God and was taken safely through the judgment. Enoch modeled a godly way of life for Methuselah. Methuselah must have passed it along to his son Lamech who shared it with his son Noah. How wonderful it is when generation after generation in one family is faithful to the Lord, especially at a time in history when violence and corruption are the normal way of life.
>
> —*Be Basic*, page 107

8. How did people pass along biblical truth from generation to generation in the time of Noah? How do believers do that today? What are some of the challenges that make it difficult to share God's truth with the next generation? What role does a changing culture play in our abilities (and our approaches) to share God's truth?

More to Consider: Read Ephesians 5:2, 8, 15 and Galatians 5:16, 25. What do these verses tell us about living a life of faith and obedience? What are the steps Noah took to follow God? What are the steps we take today? What was the result of Noah's walk? What is the result of ours?

From the Commentary

"The secret of the Lord is with them that fear him; and he will [show] them his covenant" (Ps. 25:14). When you walk with God, He speaks to you through His Word and tells you what you need to know and to do. Christians are more than just servants who do His will; we're also His friends who know His plans (John 15:14–15). God's plan involved three responsibilities for Noah and his family.

—*Be Basic*, page 108

9. What responsibilities did God give Noah and his family? (See Gen. 6:14–22.) How did Noah respond to God's call? What does this story teach us about trusting God even when He asks seemingly impossible things of us?

From the Commentary

God promised that He would never send another flood like the one He sent in Noah's day (Gen. 9:8–17). But if the flood was only a local event, God didn't keep His promise! Over the centuries, there have been numerous local floods, some of which brought death and devastation to localities. In 1996 alone, massive flooding in Afghanistan in April left 3,000 people homeless; and in July, flooding in Northern Bangladesh destroyed the homes of over 2 million people. In July and August, the Yellow, Yangtze, and Hai rivers flooded nine provinces in China and left 2,000 people dead. If Noah's flood was a local event like these floods, then God's promise and the covenant sign of the rainbow mean nothing.

The plain reading of the text convinces us that the flood was a universal judgment because "all flesh had corrupted his [God's] way upon the earth" (6:12). We don't know how far civilization had spread over the planet, but wherever humans went, there was sin that had to be judged. The flood bears witness to universal sin and universal judgment.

—Be Basic, page 113

10. Why is it critical to our theology to understand that the flood was a universal judgment? Is it possible to question the literal truth of the flood and still be a Christian? Explain. How does the Bible use the story of

the flood when talking about future events? (See Matt. 24:37–39; Luke 17:26–27; 2 Peter 3:3–7.)

Looking Inward

Take a moment to reflect on all that you've explored thus far in this study of Genesis 4:25—7:24. Review your notes and answers and think about how each of these things matters in your life today.

Tips for Small Groups: To get the most out of this section, form pairs or trios and have group members take turns answering these questions. Be honest and as open as you can in this discussion, but most of all, be encouraging and supportive of others. Be sensitive to those who are going through particularly difficult times and don't press for people to speak if they're uncomfortable doing so.

11. What are some of the best things you've been given from previous generations (not just material goods but spiritual lessons and other legacies as well)? If you have children, what are some ways you're passing the best of these things to them? What does it mean to you to leave a legacy for your children?

12. Noah obeyed God even though what God asked might have seemed impossible. What are some of the hardest things God has asked you to do? How did you respond to God when He asked you? What makes it hard to do God's will when He's asking difficult things? How can you grow more trusting in God so you can respond as Noah did?

13. In what ways is your life situation like Noah's? What are some of the worldly challenges that surround you? If you were called by God to do something as bold as what He asked Noah to do, would you do it? Why or why not?

Going Forward

14. Think of one or two things that you have learned that you'd like to work on in the coming week. Remember that this is all about quality, not quantity. It's better to work on one specific area of life and do it well than

to work on many and do poorly (or to be so overwhelmed that you simply don't try).

Do you want to learn how to better trust God's will even when it's difficult? Be specific. Go back through Genesis 4:25—7:24 and put a star next to the phrase or verse that is most encouraging to you. Consider memorizing this verse.

Real-Life Application Ideas: The first chapters of Genesis tell a story of generations. Take time in the coming week to put together a "legacy book"—something that records important teachings and truths you'd like to pass along to your children and their children. Include pictures and stories and whatever else you think will be of value for the generations to come.

Seeking Help

15. Write a prayer below (or simply pray one in silence), inviting God to work on your mind and heart in those areas you've noted in the Going Forward section. Be honest about your desires and fears.

Notes for Small Groups:

- *Look for ways to put into practice the things you wrote in the Going Forward section. Talk with other group members about your ideas and commit to being accountable to one another.*

- *During the coming week, ask the Holy Spirit to continue to reveal truth to you from what you've read and studied.*

- *Before you start the next lesson, read Genesis 8. For more in-depth lesson preparation, read chapter 9, "The God of New Beginnings," in* Be Basic.

Beginnings
(GENESIS 8)

Before you begin …
- *Pray for the Holy Spirit to reveal truth and wisdom as you go through this lesson.*
- *Read Genesis 8. This lesson references chapter 9 in* Be Basic. *It will be helpful for you to have your Bible and a copy of the commentary available as you work through this lesson.*

Getting Started

From the Commentary

When anxious believers are searching the Bible for something encouraging to read, they're more likely to turn to Romans 8 than to Genesis 8. After all, Romans 8 is one of the most heartening chapters in Scripture, while Genesis 8 describes God's "mop-up" operation after the flood.

But the next time you find yourself in a storm, Genesis 8 can give you new hope and encouragement, because the major theme of the chapter is renewal and rest after tribulation. The chapter records the end of a storm and the beginning of new life and hope for God's people and God's creation. Just consider what God does in Genesis 8 and take courage!

—*Be Basic*, page 117

1. What is the encouragement in Genesis 8? Why is it such a powerful chapter in Scripture? How can it help people who are struggling with trials?

More to Consider: How does the message in Hebrews 13:5 relate to the encouragement found in Genesis 8? Where was God when the flood covered the earth? Where is He when hope wanes?

2. Choose one verse or phrase from Genesis 8 that stands out to you. This could be something you're intrigued by, something that makes you uncomfortable, something that puzzles you, something that resonates with you, or just something you want to examine further. Write that here.

Going Deeper

From the Commentary

> Feeling forsaken is a normal human emotion that most of us have experienced, whether we admit it or not. "Why do You stand afar off, O Lord?" asked the psalmist. "Why do You hide in times of trouble?" (Ps. 10:1 NKJV). Paul confessed that his troubles in Asia had been so severe that he almost gave up on life (2 Cor. 1:8), and Jesus, who experienced all our human trials, cried from the cross, "My God, My God, why have You forsaken Me?" (Matt. 27:46 NKJV). Feeling desolate is nothing new to the people of God; but then they recall the song: "God is still on the throne, and He will remember His own!"
>
> —*Be Basic*, pages 117–18

3. What does the word *remembered* in Genesis 8:1 mean? What are other ways God remembered His people in Scripture? How does God remember believers today?

From the Commentary

> According to Genesis 7:24, the flood reached its peak in
> 150 days. The torrential rain and the eruptions of water
> from beneath the earth had both ceased (8:2; see NIV and
> NASB), and during the next five months, God caused the
> water to recede and leave the dry land behind.
>
> Where did the floodwaters go? Never underestimate the
> power of moving water! It's possible that the flood greatly
> altered the contours of the land and created new areas
> for the water to fill, both on the surface of the earth and
> underground. Since there were eruptions from beneath
> the earth (7:11), whole continents and mountain ranges
> could have risen and fallen, creating huge areas into
> which the water could spill. The winds that God sent over
> the earth helped to evaporate the water and also move it
> to the places God had provided. A God powerful enough
> to cover the earth with water is also wise enough to know
> how to dispose of it when its work is done.
>
> —*Be Basic*, pages 119–20

4. Review Genesis 8:1–14. What does this passage reveal about God's
power? About God's plan? How does God reshape people like He reshapes
the contours of the earth?

From the History Books

Since the third century AD, intrepid adventurers have sought to determine the final resting place of Noah's ark. Genesis 8:4 describes the resting place as "the mountains of Ararat," so expeditions typically focus their search efforts on this location in modern-day Turkey, in hopes of discovering evidence of the iconic boat. The discovery of Noah's ark is such a prize that it has led to many hoaxes from people hoping to cash in on the gullibility of hopeful Christians. So far, no concrete physical evidence has been found to prove the existence of the ark.

5. Why is the ark such a prize for researchers? What do they hope to prove if they find the ark? How might scientific evidence of an ark from Noah's time affect the beliefs of Christians? Of non-Christians? How does the lack of evidence affect Christians' beliefs?

From the Commentary

The Hebrew text says that "the ark came to rest," reminding us that Noah's name means "rest" and that his father Lamech had hoped that his son would bring rest to a weary world (Gen. 5:28–29). Though the ark had rested safely, Noah was waiting for the Lord to tell him what to do. He waited forty days and then sent out the raven; and being an unclean carrion-eating bird (Lev. 11:13–15), it felt right at home among the floating carcasses.

Noah waited a week and then sent out a dove, which, being a clean bird, found no place to land; so it returned to the ark (Gen. 8:8–9). A week later Noah sent the dove out again, and when it returned with a fresh olive leaf, Noah knew that the plants were growing and fresh life had appeared on the earth (vv. 10–11). A dove bearing an olive branch is a familiar symbol of peace around the world. A week later, when Noah sent the dove out the third time, it didn't return; so he knew the water had dried up.

—*Be Basic*, page 120

6. What's significant about Noah's decision to wait after the ark came to rest? How did Noah show his trust in God by sending the raven, then the dove? What is the overall message in this passage for us today?

From the Commentary

> Noah was a man of faith whose name is recorded in
> Hebrews 11 with those of other heroes of faith (v. 7).
> He had the faith to walk with God when the people of
> the world were ignoring and disobeying God. He had
> the faith to work for God and to witness for God when
> opposition to truth was the popular thing. Now that the
> flood was over, he exercised faith to wait on God before
> leaving the ark.
>
> After being confined to the ark for over a year, he and his
> family must have yearned to get back on dry land, but
> they waited for God's directions. Circumstances on the
> earth looked suitable for their disembarking, but that was
> no guarantee that God wanted them to exit immediately
> and begin their new life.
>
> —*Be Basic*, page 121

7. Review Genesis 8:15–19. Did Noah reveal unbelief when he sent out the
birds or opened the hatch to look at the terrain? Why or why not? Read
Romans 10:17. How does this verse speak to Noah's faith?

From the Commentary

> What was it that caused the population to reject God's word and perish? ... They believed that life would go on as it always had and that nothing would change. They said that God wouldn't invade the world or interrupt the scheme of things, but He did! People today have the same attitude concerning the return of the Lord (2 Peter 3:1–9; 1 Thess. 5:1–10).
>
> When it comes to saving faith, each of us must trust Jesus Christ personally; we can't be saved by the faith of a substitute.
>
> —*Be Basic*, page 122

8. How were the people of Noah's day who didn't follow God like the people described in Luke 14:16–24 and Matthew 24:36–41? How do such people explain their behavior? What makes sense about their explanations? What are the flaws of their reasoning?

More to Consider: In Old Testament days, when you sacrificed a burnt offering, you gave the entire animal or bird to the Lord with nothing kept back. How was the way Noah gave himself and his family to God a similar act of sacrifice? What was God's response to their trust in Him?

From the Commentary

> The Lord didn't speak the words in Genesis 8:21–22 to Noah; He spoke them to Himself in His own heart. It was His gracious response to Noah's faith, obedience, and worship. What did God promise?
>
> The ground cursed no more (v. 21a).
>
> No more universal floods (v. 21b).
>
> No interruption of the cycle of nature (v. 22).
>
> —*Be Basic*, pages 124–25

9. What's significant about each of God's promises in Genesis 8:21–22? Does this mean God wouldn't punish evil from that day forward? Why or why not? How do these promises still allow for God's justice to prevail?

From the Commentary

The guarantee in Genesis 8:22 gives us hope and courage as we face an unknown future. Each time we go to bed for the night, or turn the calendar to a new month, we should be reminded that God is concerned about planet earth and its inhabitants. With the invention of the electric light and modern means of transportation and communication, our world has moved away from living by the cycles of nature established by God. We no longer go to bed at sundown and get up at sunrise, and if we don't like the weather where we are, we can quickly travel to a different climate. But if God were to dim the sun, rearrange the seasons, or tilt the earth at a different angle, our lives would be in jeopardy.

God invites us to live a day at a time. Jesus taught us to pray, "Give us this day our daily bread" (Matt. 6:11) and to be thankful for it. "As your days, so shall your strength be" (Deut. 33:25 NKJV; see Matt. 6:25–34). When His disciples warned Jesus not to go to Bethany, He replied, "Are there not twelve hours in the day?" (John 11:9). He obeyed the Father's schedule and lived a day at a time, trusting the Father to care for Him.

—*Be Basic*, page 126

10. God's promise that He wouldn't send another flood was assurance to the Jews that His covenant with them would never be broken, and yet the Jews broke the covenant over and over again. What does this tell us about

God's character? About humanity's character? What hope should the Jews have found in the message of Genesis 8:22? What does that hope look like for Christians today?

Looking Inward

Take a moment to reflect on all that you've explored thus far in this study of Genesis 8. Review your notes and answers and think about how each of these things matters in your life today.

> *Tips for Small Groups: To get the most out of this section, form pairs or trios and have group members take turns answering these questions. Be honest and as open as you can in this discussion, but most of all, be encouraging and supportive of others. Be sensitive to those who are going through particularly difficult times and don't press for people to speak if they're uncomfortable doing so.*

11. Noah may have felt a little lost and forsaken after the ark rested on the mountain. Have you ever felt led somewhere by God only to be left (apparently) alone? How did you deal with that feeling of being forsaken? What was God teaching you in that time?

12. Is it important to you that science finds evidence of biblical events (such as the ark)? Why or why not? What would the discovery of the ark do for your faith?

13. Noah's story is ultimately one of hope. What are some of the ways it inspires you? What are some of the things you hope for? How can Noah's faithfulness help you to trust God in those areas of life?

Going Forward

14. Think of one or two things that you have learned that you'd like to work on in the coming week. Remember that this is all about quality, not quantity. It's better to work on one specific area of life and do it well than to work on many and do poorly (or to be so overwhelmed that you simply don't try).

Do you want to learn how to wait on God in the times when He seems distant? Be specific. Go back through Genesis 8 and put a star next to the phrase or verse that is most encouraging to you. Consider memorizing this verse.

Real-Life Application Ideas: Noah's name means "rest." When the ark came to rest atop the mountain, he and his family enjoyed a sort of forced rest until the dove returned with an olive branch. Look for a way to give your own family a time of rest. During this time, avoid the common distractions of TV and the Internet, and instead, spend time enjoying each other and listening to God.

Seeking Help

15. Write a prayer below (or simply pray one in silence), inviting God to work on your mind and heart in those areas you've noted in the Going Forward section. Be honest about your desires and fears.

Notes for Small Groups:

- *Look for ways to put into practice the things you wrote in the Going Forward section. Talk with other group members about your ideas and commit to being accountable to one another.*

- *During the coming week, ask the Holy Spirit to continue to reveal truth to you from what you've read and studied.*

- *Before you start the next lesson, read Genesis 9—10. For more in-depth lesson preparation, read chapters 10 and 11, "To Life! To Life!" and "The Rest of the Story,"* in Be Basic.

The Rest of the Story

(GENESIS 9—10)

Before you begin …

- *Pray for the Holy Spirit to reveal truth and wisdom as you go through this lesson.*
- *Read Genesis 9—10. This lesson references chapters 10 and 11 in* Be Basic. *It will be helpful for you to have your Bible and a copy of the commentary available as you work through this lesson.*

Getting Started

From the Commentary

When Noah came out of the ark, he was like a "second Adam" about to usher in a new beginning on earth for the human race. Faith in the Lord had saved Noah and his household from destruction, and his three sons would repopulate the whole earth (Gen. 9:18).

God had told Adam and Eve to "be fruitful, and multiply, and replenish the earth" (1:28), and He repeated that mandate *twice* to Noah and his family (9:1, 7). All of Noah's descendants were important to the plan of God, but especially the line of Shem. From that line Abraham would be born, the man God chose to found the Jewish nation. From that nation would come the Redeemer who would fulfill 3:15 and crush the serpent's head.

In Scripture, children are described as a blessing, not a curse, and to have many children and grandchildren was evidence of the favor of God (Gen. 24:60; Ps. 127:3–5; 128:3–4). God promised Abraham that his descendants would be as the stars of the sky and the sand of the sea (Gen. 15:5; 22:17), and the patriarchs invoked the blessing of fruitfulness on their heirs (28:3; 35:11; 48:4). The Lord covenanted with Israel to give them many children if the nation would obey His laws (Lev. 26:9; Deut. 7:13).

—*Be Basic*, pages 129–30

1. Review Genesis 9:1–7. How are modern attitudes about children different from those espoused by Noah and the godly generations that followed him? How was God's message to Noah to "be fruitful and increase in number" ultimately a message about God's love? In what ways is this message still true today?

More to Consider: A survey taken in 1900 revealed that people felt they needed seventy-two things in order to function normally and be content. Fifty years later, in a similar survey, the total came to nearly five hundred things! Genesis 9:2–4 talks about God's provision for His people. What does 1 Timothy 6:8 tell us are the only things we need to function?

2. Choose one verse or phrase from Genesis 9—10 that stands out to you. This could be something you're intrigued by, something that makes you uncomfortable, something that puzzles you, something that resonates with you, or just something you want to examine further. Write that here.

Going Deeper

From the Commentary

From instructing Noah about the shedding of animal blood, the Lord proceeded to discuss an even more important topic: the shedding of human blood. Thus far, mankind didn't have a very good track record when it came to caring for one another. Cain had killed his brother Abel (Gen. 4:8), Lamech had killed a young man and bragged about it (vv. 23–24), and the earth had been filled with all kinds of violence (6:11, 13). God had put the fear of humans into the animals, but now He had to put the fear of God into the humans lest they destroy one another!

Those who kill their fellow human beings will have to answer to God for their deeds, for men and women are made in the image of God. To attack a human being is to attack God, and the Lord will bring judgment on the offender. All life is the gift of God, and to take away life means to take the place of God. The Lord gives life and He alone has the right to authorize taking it away (Job 1:21).

—*Be Basic*, page 132

3. Read James 4:1–3. What are the roots of violence? How did God arrange to punish murderers and see that justice is done and the law upheld? (See Gen. 9:6.) Why is human life so important to God?

From the Commentary

> Genesis 9:8–17 is the section theologians call "The
> Noahic Covenant." Though God spoke especially to
> Noah and his sons, this covenant includes all of Noah's
> descendants (v. 9) and "all generations to come" (v. 12
> NIV). The covenant doesn't stop there, however, for it
> also includes every living creature (vv. 10, 12) and "all
> living creatures of every kind" (v. 15 NIV). Humans, birds,
> beasts, and wild animals are encompassed in this wonder-
> ful covenant.
>
> —*Be Basic*, page 134

4. What did God promise in this covenant (Gen. 9:8–17)? Why didn't He
lay down conditions that humans had to obey? What was the main point
of this covenant?

From the Commentary

> God spoke of the rainbow as though Noah and his fam-
> ily were familiar with it, so it must have existed before

the flood. Rainbows are caused by the sunlight filtering through the water in the air, each drop becoming a prism to release the colors hidden in the white light of the sun. Rainbows are fragile but beautiful, and nobody has to pay to see them! Their lovely colors speak to us of what Peter called "the manifold grace of God" (1 Peter 4:10). The Greek word translated "manifold" means "various, many-colored, variegated." The rainbow reminds us of God's gracious covenant and the "many-colored" grace of God.

God hasn't promised that we'll never experience storms, but He has promised that the storms won't destroy us. "When you pass through the waters, I will be with you; and through the rivers, they shall not overflow you" (Isa. 43:2 NKJV). When the clouds appear and the sun is hidden, we have nothing to fear.

But the rainbow isn't only for us to see, for the Lord said, "I will look upon it" (Gen. 9:16). Certainly God doesn't forget His covenants with His people, but this is just another way of assuring us that we don't need to be afraid. When we look at the rainbow, we know that our Father is also looking at the rainbow, and therefore it becomes a bridge that brings us together.

—*Be Basic*, pages 135–36

5. In Genesis 9:16, the Lord said He would look upon rainbows when they appeared. Why is it notable that He said the rainbow isn't just for people? What was the rainbow supposed to remind us of? Why do we sometimes fret and worry despite this promise?

From the Commentary

The index for "the rest of the story" is in Genesis 9:18–19. The main characters are listed—Noah, Shem, Ham, and Japheth—and the main theme of this section is announced: how Noah's family multiplied and scattered over the earth. A contemporary reader of the Bible is tempted to skip these lists of obscure names, but that doesn't minimize their importance. These "obscure people" founded the nations that throughout Bible history interacted with each other and helped to accomplish God's purposes on this earth. The descendants of Shem—the people of Israel—have played an especially important part on the stage of history.

—*Be Basic*, page 142

6. Review Genesis 9:18–23. Why does the Bible include so many lists of obscure people? What is the point of the lists? What does it say about God? About His people?

From the Commentary

> In becoming a farmer, Noah followed the vocation of his
> father Lamech (Gen. 5:28–29). While the Bible condemns
> drunkenness, it doesn't condemn the growing or eating of
> grapes or the drinking of wine. Grapes, raisins, and wine
> were important elements in the diet of Eastern peoples.
> In fact, in Old Testament society, wine was considered a
> blessing from God (Ps. 104:14–15; Deut. 14:26) and was
> even used with the sacrifices (Lev. 23:13; Num. 28:7).
>
> This is the first mention of wine in Scripture, but
> wine-making was practiced before the flood, and Noah
> certainly knew what too much wine would do to him. In
> an attempt to exonerate Noah, some students claim that
> the flood brought about a change in the earth's atmo-
> sphere, and this caused the grape juice to ferment for the
> first time, but the defense is feeble. Noah had picked the
> grapes, crushed them in the winepress, put the juice into
> skins, and waited for the juice to ferment.
>
> Both his drunkenness and his nakedness were disgrace-
> ful, and the two often go together (Gen. 19:30–38; Hab.
> 2:15–16; Lam. 4:21). Alcohol isn't a stimulant, it's a
> narcotic; and when the brain is affected by alcohol, the
> person loses self-control. At least Noah was in his own
> tent when this happened and not out in public. But when
> you consider who he was (a preacher of righteousness) and
> what he had done (saved his household from death), his
> sin becomes even more repulsive.
>
> —*Be Basic*, pages 142–43

7. Read the following passages: Proverbs 20:1; 23:19–21, 29–35; Isaiah 5:11; Habakkuk 2:15; Romans 13:13; 1 Corinthians 6:10; Ephesians 5:18. What do they say about drunkenness? Why is this considered a sin? What made Noah's sin worth recording in Scripture? What does this reveal about the nature of humankind? About the role of redemption and forgiveness?

From the Commentary

Ham shouldn't have entered his father's tent without an invitation. Did he call to his father and receive no answer? Did he wonder if Noah was sick or perhaps even dead? Did he even know that his father had been drinking wine? These are questions the text doesn't answer, so it's useless for us to speculate. One thing is certain: Ham was disrespectful to his father in what he did.

Ham could have peeked into the tent, quickly sized up the situation, and covered his father's body, saying nothing about the incident to anyone. Instead, he seems to have enjoyed the sight and then told his two brothers about it in a rather disrespectful manner. He may even have suggested that they go take a look for themselves.

Moses hadn't yet said, "Honor your father and your mother" (Ex. 20:12 NIV), but surely the impulse is natural to children and should have been present in Ham's heart.

—*Be Basic*, pages 143–44

8. How is the way people respond to the sin and embarrassment of others an indication of their character? Why did Ham show such disrespect to his father? What was God's response to Ham's action?

More to Consider: How did Shem and Japheth show their love for their father by practicing the truth found in Proverbs 10:12? (See also 1 Peter 4:8.) Read Proverbs 17:9 and 12:16. How do these verses apply to this story? What is the takeaway from this story for us today?

From the Commentary

When Noah awakened from his drunken stupor, he was probably ashamed of what he had done, but he was also surprised to find himself covered by a garment. Naturally, he wondered what had happened in the tent while he was asleep. The logical thing would be to speak to Japheth, his firstborn, and he and Shem must have told him what Ham had done.

The words in Genesis 9:24–29 are Noah's only recorded speech found in Scripture. It's too bad that this brief speech has been misunderstood and labeled a "curse," because what Noah said is more like a father's prophecy concerning his children and grandchildren. The word "curse" is used only once, but it's directed at Ham's youngest son Canaan and not at Ham himself. This suggests that Noah was describing the future of his sons and one grandson on the basis of what he saw in their character, not unlike what Jacob did before he died (Gen. 49).

Noah lived another three-and-a-half centuries, and we have every reason to believe that he walked with God and served Him faithfully. As far as the record is concerned, he fell once, and certainly he repented and the Lord forgave him. In our walk with God, we climb the hills and sometimes we descend into the valleys. As Alexander Whyte used to say, "The victorious Christian life is a series of new beginnings."

—*Be Basic*, pages 144–45, 47

9. Review Genesis 9:24–29. Why do some people label these words a "curse"? Is it notable that these are the only recorded words of Noah in Scripture? Why or why not? What can Noah's life (obedience, then sin,

followed by apparent obedience again) teach us about how we ought to live?

From the Commentary

Genesis 10 is known as "The Table of Nations" and is unique in the annals of ancient history. The purpose of the chapter is given at the beginning (v. 1) and the end (v. 32): to explain how the earth was repopulated after the flood by the descendants of the three sons of Noah. You find a similar (but not identical) listing in 1 Chronicles 1.

Before we look at some of the details of this chapter, and then try to draw some spiritual lessons from it, we need to heed some warnings.

First, the listing is not a typical genealogy that gives only the names of descendants. The writer reminds us that these ancient peoples had their own "clans and languages ... territories and nations" (Gen. 10:31 NIV). In other words, this is a genealogy plus an atlas plus a history book. We're watching the movements of people and nations in the ancient world.

Second, the listing isn't complete. For example, we don't find Edom, Moab, and Ammon mentioned, and yet these were important nations in biblical history. The fact that there are seventy nations in the list suggests that the arrangement may be deliberately artificial, an approach often used in writing such listings. There were seventy persons in Jacob's family when they went to Egypt (Gen. 46:27; Ex. 1:5), and our Lord sent approximately seventy disciples out to preach the Word (Luke 10:1).

Third, it's difficult to identify some of these nations and give them "modern" names. Over the centuries, nations can change their names, move to different locations, modify their language, and even alter their racial composition through intermarriage.

—*Be Basic*, pages 147–48

10. How might Genesis 9—10 have been an encouragement to the people of Israel when they conquered Canaan? What legacies did Noah's sons leave the world? How is this like or unlike the legacies other biblical characters left? What are some of the lessons we learn about God from the life of Noah and his legacy?

Looking Inward

Take a moment to reflect on all that you've explored thus far in this study of Genesis 9—10. Review your notes and answers and think about how each of these things matters in your life today.

Tips for Small Groups: To get the most out of this section, form pairs or trios and have group members take turns answering these questions. Be honest and as open as you can in this discussion, but most of all, be encouraging and supportive of others. Be sensitive to those who are going through particularly difficult times and don't press for people to speak if they're uncomfortable doing so.

11. It doesn't take long for violence and murder to enter the human story. What causes people to choose violence over alternative resolution options? What kinds of things tempt you to violence? If you've ever been the victim of violence, how did you deal with that situation?

12. God promises Noah that He will never flood the whole earth again, but He doesn't promise there won't be storms. What are some of the personal storms you've endured recently? Did they feel like floods? How do you deal

with the challenges that storms bring into your life? Where do you find God in the midst of those times?

13. How do you react when you see someone else's sin? Are you ever tempted to publicize it? How does God want you to respond when you observe someone else's sin?

Going Forward

14. Think of one or two things that you have learned that you'd like to work on in the coming week. Remember that this is all about quality, not quantity. It's better to work on one specific area of life and do it well than to work on many and do poorly (or to be so overwhelmed that you simply don't try).

Do you want to learn how to leave a good legacy? Be specific. Go back through Genesis 9—10 and put a star next to the phrase or verse that is most encouraging to you. Consider memorizing this verse.

Real-Life Application Ideas: You don't have to look very far to find evidence of people's sinfulness. As you reflect on the choices people have made—whether family members or coworkers or church members or people who live in the public eye—instead of gossiping about their sin, spend time in prayer for them. Learn from the examples of Shem and Japheth and show respect for those who, like you, are imperfect people.

Seeking Help

15. Write a prayer below (or simply pray one in silence), inviting God to work on your mind and heart in those areas you've noted in the Going Forward section. Be honest about your desires and fears.

Notes for Small Groups:

- *Look for ways to put into practice the things you wrote in the Going Forward section. Talk with other group members about your ideas and commit to being accountable to one another.*

- *During the coming week, ask the Holy Spirit to continue to reveal truth to you from what you've read and studied.*

- *Before you start the next lesson, read Genesis 11. For more in-depth lesson preparation, read chapter 12, "Caution—God at Work," and if time, read chapter 13, "Back to Basics," which is a review of Genesis 1—11, in* Be Basic.

God at Work

(GENESIS 11)

Before you begin …

- *Pray for the Holy Spirit to reveal truth and wisdom as you go through this lesson.*
- *Read Genesis 11. This lesson references chapters 12 and 13 in* Be Basic. *It will be helpful for you to have your Bible and a copy of the commentary available as you work through this lesson.*

Getting Started

From the Commentary

"Man proposes, but God disposes."

That familiar statement is almost a religious cliché. Many people who use it don't even know what it means. It was written by the Augustinian monk Thomas à Kempis (ca. 1380–1471) in his classic book *On the Imitation of Christ.* An expanded version is the proverb, "Man does what he can, God does what He will." Solomon used more words but said it best: "There are many plans in a man's heart, nevertheless the Lord's counsel—that will stand" (Prov. 19:21 NKJV).

Few chapters in the Bible illustrate this truth better than Genesis 11.

—*Be Basic*, page 153

1. How does the story of Babel reveal God's hand in the world? What does it teach us about God's plan and purposes?

2. Choose one verse or phrase from Genesis 11 that stands out to you. This could be something you're intrigued by, something that makes you uncomfortable, something that puzzles you, something that resonates with you, or just something you want to examine further. Write that here.

Going Deeper

From the Commentary

It's likely that the events in Genesis chapter 11 occurred prior to those in chapter 10 and that the scattering described in chapter 10 was the consequence of God's judgment at Babel. Perhaps the story was placed here in Genesis so it could lead into the genealogy of Shem which leads into the genealogy of Abraham, the founder of the Hebrew nation. The arrangement, then, is literary and not chronological.

God had commanded the peoples to be fruitful and multiply and to scatter across the earth, but they decided to move to Nimrod's city of Babylon and settle there (11:1–12). This move was blatant rebellion against God's command that the people scatter. Apparently Nimrod wanted them in his cities and under his control.

The "tower" that they built at Babel was what is known as a "ziggurat." Archeologists have excavated several of these large structures which were built primarily for religious purposes. A ziggurat was like a pyramid except that the successive levels were recessed so that you could walk to the top on "steps." At the top was a special shrine dedicated to a god or goddess. In building the structure, the people weren't trying to climb up to heaven to dethrone God; rather, they hoped that the god or goddess they worshipped would come down from heaven to meet them. The structure and the city were called "Babel," which means "the gate of the gods."

—*Be Basic*, page 154

3. Review Genesis 11:1–4. Why did the people disobey God's command to scatter and repopulate the earth? (Compare this to the Devil's temptation in Genesis 3:5.) In what ways was the building of the tower a declaration of war against God? (See also Ps. 2:1–3.) In what ways was it merely a show of arrogance?

From the Commentary

"Whom the gods would destroy," wrote historian Charles Beard, "they first make mad with power." From Babel to Belshazzar (Dan. 5), and from Herod (Acts 12:20–25) to Hitler, God has demonstrated repeatedly that it doesn't pay to rebel against His will. "Pride goes before destruction, and a haughty spirit before a fall" (Prov. 16:18 NKJV), and Jesus warned that those who exalt themselves will be abased (Matt. 23:12).

God in heaven is never perplexed or paralyzed by what people do on earth. Babel's conceited "Let's go up!" was answered by heaven's calm "Let's go down!" "He who sits in the heavens shall laugh; the Lord shall hold them in derision" (Ps. 2:4 NKJV). Of course, God doesn't have to

investigate to know what's going on in His universe; the
language is used only to dramatize God's intervention.

—*Be Basic*, page 155

4. Review God's response in Genesis 11:5–9. How did God's judgment
speak to both the immediate circumstance and the future concerns? Why
was the "unity of humankind" a false sense of power? How is this different
from "unity in Christ" that Paul preached about in the New Testament?

More to Consider: The word babel *sounds like the Hebrew word*
balal, *which means "confusion" or "disorder." Review 1 Corinthians
14:33. What does this verse teach us about the source of "confusion" in
our world? What is God's response to the world's confusion?*

From Today's World

Babylon in biblical times wasn't just a geographical location, it was also a
symbol of worldliness and sin. The tower of Babel is just one example of
the kind of godlessness that persisted back in the early days of humankind.
Today, Babylon is more of an idea or a philosophy than a place, though

some might be quick to point to Hollywood (or Wall Street, depending on whom you ask) when pressed to answer "What is today's Babylon?" But you don't have to live and walk in Hollywood to experience the muck and mire of worldliness; it's evident all across the globe (and more readily accessible than ever, thanks to the Internet).

5. What are some other examples of modern-day Babylon in society today? What is it about worldliness that's so tempting for people? What are some of the ways our culture aspires to "build a tower" in defiance of God? How do we differentiate between selfishness and success?

From the Commentary

> In the original Babel, the people wanted to build a tower that reached up to heaven, but in the Babylon of Revelation 17—18, Babylon's sins reach up to heaven (18:5). The original worldwide unity that Nimrod desired for the Genesis Babylon will one day be achieved by Satan's godless world system (17:3, 9, 11, 23). Earthly Babylon is called a prostitute, while the Holy City from heaven is called bride of Christ (17:1–2; 21:9ff.).

"Every generation builds its own towers," writes psycho-therapist Naomi H. Rosenblatt, and she is right. Whether these are actual skyscrapers (the Willis Tower [formerly Sears] and Tribune Tower in Chicago, the Eiffel Tower in Paris, the Trump Tower in New York City), or mega-corporations that circle the globe, the idea is the same: "We will make a name for ourselves." God's people can't escape being in the world, because it's in the world that we have our ministry, but we must avoid being of the world. We're not here to build the arrogant towers of men; we're here to help build the church of Jesus Christ.

—*Be Basic*, page 157

6. What are the limits of humankind's abilities? What did God accomplish that humans could not? Why is unity apart from Christ not unity at all?

From the Commentary

God had promised that He would send a Redeemer, the seed of the woman (Gen. 3:15), who would defeat Satan and bring salvation. Noah's prophecy revealed that God would bless the world through the line of Shem, the "Semites" who were the ancestors of the Hebrew people (9:26–27). "Shem was the ancestor of all the sons of Eber" (10:21 NIV), and it's likely that the word "Hebrew" comes from the name "Eber."

Genesis gives us two genealogies of Shem, in 10:21–29 and in 11:10–26. The first genealogy lists all five of his sons and five of his grandsons, but then it focuses on the descendants of Arphaxad: Shelah, Eber, and Eber's two sons Peleg and Joktan. It lists Joktan's many sons but ignores Peleg's descendants. But the genealogy in chapter 11 picks up Peleg's side of the family and takes us through to Abraham. The genealogy in Genesis 5 takes us from Adam to Noah, and the one in Genesis 11 goes from Noah's son Shem to Terah and his son Abraham.

Except that both lists have ten generations, the listing in 11:10–26 is different from the genealogy in Genesis 5. For one thing, it doesn't contain the repeated phrase "and he died." The emphasis is on how old the man was at the birth of his firstborn son. The people named in 11:10–26 didn't live as long as the men named in Genesis 5. The list begins with Noah's 950 years and dwindles down to Nahor's 148 years. The post-flood generations were starting to feel the physical consequences of sin in the human body.

—Be Basic, pages 158–59

7. Review Genesis 11:10–26. What's the most important thing to glean from this genealogy? What does it reveal about God's promises? About the way God watches over His people? In what ways are the genealogies in the Bible bridges that lead us to redemption?

From the Commentary

> If Genesis 1—11 is a record of four key events—creation, the fall, the flood, and the judgment at Babel—then Genesis 12—50 is the record of the lives of four key men: Abraham, Isaac, Jacob, and Joseph. In 11:27–32, five persons stand out: Abraham and his wife Sarah; Terah, Abraham's father; and Nahor and Haran, Abraham's brothers. Haran died and left his son Lot behind.
>
> It was God's purpose to call a man and his wife and from them build a family. From that family He would build a nation, and from that nation, God would bless all the nations of the earth (12:1–3; 18:18).
>
> —*Be Basic*, page 159

8. How is God's decision to build a nation from a family (Abraham's line) an act of grace? What sort of upbringing did Abraham and Sarah have (Josh. 24:2)? What does this teach us about the kind of people God can use to accomplish His purposes?

From the Commentary

The remarkable thing about God's call of Abraham and Sarah was that they were childless. Abram means "exalted father," but he wasn't a father at all! They were the least likely candidates to have a family and build a great nation. But God's ways are not our ways (Isa. 55:8–9), and by calling and blessing a barren couple, the Lord revealed the greatness of His power and His glory. Abram would be named "Abraham," which means "father of many nations."

We live in a confused world and Babel is still with us. But God still has His faithful remnant that follows Him by faith and keeps their eyes on the heavenly city (Heb. 11:13–16).

—*Be Basic*, page 160

9. Compare and contrast the ways of the people in Babylon with Abraham and Sarah's journey. How does the world accomplish things differently from the way God accomplishes them? Where did the world get its wisdom? Where did Abraham and Sarah get theirs? (See Heb. 11:11–12.)

From the Commentary

The Bible opens with a declaration that God exists: "In the beginning God" (Gen. 1:1). Genesis presents no philosophical arguments to prove God's existence; it just puts Him at the beginning of everything. When you open your Bible, God is there, and He was there before the Bible was written or even the universe was created.

The God you meet in Genesis 1—11 is not only eternal, but He's also wise and powerful. He is a great God, and so great is His power that He only has to speak to make things happen. And so great is His wisdom that what He creates is to be—and it works! From the tiniest one-celled animal to the biggest galaxy, in all creation God's power and wisdom are manifested.

And yet this great God is a personal God. He pays attention to us and wants to be our Lord and our Friend!

He is a holy God who will not condone sin. He judged the personal sins of Adam, Eve, and Cain, and also the corporate sins of the antediluvian population and the people at Babel. But at the same time, He is a God of love who created us in His image and longs to fellowship with us and reveal Himself to us. Our sins grieve Him, but in His grace, He forgives those who trust Him and will give them another chance.

—*Be Basic*, pages 163–64

10. List some of the attributes of God you noticed while reading Genesis. In what ways do these first eleven chapters reveal God's plan for humankind? What promises does God make in these chapters? In what ways do the events in these chapters prepare the way for Jesus?

Looking Inward

Take a moment to reflect on all that you've explored thus far in this study of Genesis 11. Review your notes and answers and think about how each of these things matters in your life today.

Tips for Small Groups: To get the most out of this section, form pairs or trios and have group members take turns answering these questions. Be honest and as open as you can in this discussion, but most of all, be encouraging and supportive of others. Be sensitive to those who are going through particularly difficult times and don't press for people to speak if they're uncomfortable doing so.

11. The Tower of Babel symbolized humanity's arrogance. Have you ever felt like you knew better than God? Describe that situation. What were the results? What are the things that tempt you to become arrogant? How can you learn to trust God more when confronted with those temptations?

12. What is your "Babylon" today? Where do you most struggle with worldliness? What would your life look like if you were less worldly? How can you improve in this area?

13. Abraham and Sarah (Abram and Sarai) are introduced at the end of these first eleven chapters in Genesis. What strikes you as most notable about their character? Why does God choose a barren couple from which to build His nation? What are some of the ways God has used your weakness or apparent deficiency to accomplish His purposes?

Going Forward

14. Think of one or two things that you have learned that you'd like to work on in the coming week. Remember that this is all about quality, not quantity. It's better to work on one specific area of life and do it well than to work on many and do poorly (or to be so overwhelmed that you simply don't try).

Do you want to learn how to avoid worldliness? Be specific. Go back through Genesis 11 and put a star next to the phrase or verse that is most encouraging to you. Consider memorizing this verse.

Real-Life Application Ideas: Take a close look at the habits and choices that define you. Look for any appearance of worldliness. How do you know when you're trusting the wisdom (or following the foolishness) of other people instead of God? Work this week on eliminating worldly endeavors in favor of following God. This may not be easy in some areas of life—we live in the world, after all—but it's a good way to sort through what matters most to you and turn your attention toward God rather than the temptations of the world.

Seeking Help

15. Write a prayer below (or simply pray one in silence), inviting God to work on your mind and heart in those areas you've noted in the Going Forward section. Be honest about your desires and fears.

Notes for Small Groups:

- *Look for ways to put into practice the things you wrote in the Going Forward section. Talk with other group members about your ideas and commit to being accountable to one another.*

- *During the coming week, ask the Holy Spirit to continue to reveal truth to you from what you've read and studied.*

- *Read chapter 13 in* Be Basic *if you didn't have time to do so before this lesson.*

Summary and Review

Notes for Small Groups: This session is a summary and review of this book. Because of that, it is shorter than the previous lessons. If you are using this in a small-group setting, consider combining this lesson with a time of fellowship or a shared meal.

Before you begin …
- *Pray for the Holy Spirit to reveal truth and wisdom as you go through this lesson.*
- *Briefly review the notes you made in the previous sessions. You will refer back to previous sections throughout this bonus lesson.*

Looking Back

1. Over the past eight lessons, you've examined the first eleven chapters of Genesis. What expectations did you bring to this study? In what ways were those expectations met?

2. What is the most significant personal discovery you've made from this study?

3. What surprised you most about God's role in the lives of the first humans? What, if anything, troubled you?

Progress Report

4. Take a few moments to review the Going Forward sections of the previous lessons. How would you rate your progress for each of the things you chose to work on? What adjustments, if any, do you need to make to continue on the path toward spiritual maturity?

5. In what ways have you grown closer to Christ during this study? Take a moment to celebrate those things. Then think of areas where you feel you still need to grow and note those here. Make plans to revisit this study in a few weeks to review your growing faith.

Things to Pray About

6. Genesis 1—11 focuses on beginnings and humankind's first rebellion against God. As you reflect on how God responds to humans' choices, think about how you are like and unlike the characters in Genesis 1—11. What can you learn from their choices (both good and bad) that can help you grow closer to God?

7. The messages in Genesis 1—11 focus on God's love, people's selfishness, the introduction of sin, the hope for the future, and God's ultimate plan for humankind. Spend time praying about each of these topics.

8. Whether you've been studying this in a small group or on your own, there are many other Christians working through the very same issues you discovered when examining these first chapters of Genesis. Take time to pray for them, that God would reveal truth, that the Holy Spirit would guide you, and that each person might grow in spiritual maturity according to God's will.

A Blessing of Encouragement

Studying the Bible is one of the best ways to learn how to be more like Christ. Thanks for taking this step. In closing, let this blessing precede you and follow you into the next week while you continue to marinate in God's Word:

May God light your path to greater understanding as you review the truths found in Genesis 1—11 and consider how they can help you grow closer to Christ.

The "BE" series . . .

For years pastors and lay leaders have embraced Warren W. Wiersbe's very accessible commentary of the Bible through the individual "BE" series. Through the work of David C Cook Global Mission, the "BE" series is part of a library of books made available to indigenous Christian workers. These are men and women who are called by God to grow the kingdom through their work with the local church worldwide. Here are a few of their remarks as to how Dr. Wiersbe's writings have benefited their ministry.

"Most Christian books I see are priced too high for me . . .
I received a collection that included 12 Wiersbe
commentaries a few months ago and I have
read every one of them.
I use them for my personal devotions every day and they
are incredibly helpful for preparing sermons.
The contribution David C Cook is making to the
church in India is amazing."
—Pastor E. M. Abraham, Hyderabad, India